319044

This book is to be returned

AT HOME

First published by Hodder Children's Books in 2006

Reprinted in 2006

Editor: Kirsty Hamilton
Designer: Peter Bailey, Proof Books

British Library Cataloguing in Publication Data
Llewellyn, Claire
Look out at home
1.Home accidents – Prevention – Pictorial works – Juvenile literature
I.Title II.Gordon, Mike III.At home
613.6

Printed in China

ISBN-10: 0340 894431
ISBN-13: 978 0 3408 9443 9

Hodder Children's Books
A division of Hodder Headline Limited
338 Euston Road,
London NW1 3BH

LOOK OUT!
AT HOME

Written by Claire Llewellyn

Illustrated by Mike Gordon

Hodder
Children's
Books

a division of Hodder Headline Limited

Home is where you live with your family. It's a very special place.

Spot

5

Home is where you play your favourite games.

It's comfortable and safe. Or is it?

6

Have you ever slipped on
a toy or gone
bump
    bump
        bump
            down the stairs?

Perhaps home is not always as safe as it seems.

Thank goodness someone's usually around to keep an eye on you.

But what if Mum's busy,
or Dad's on the phone?

Can you take care of yourself?

Some things around the house
are sharp.

Sharp things are useful
for cutting things.

Sharp
scissors →

Sharp
knife →

Sharp
saw ↓

But what could happen if
you played with them?

Many things in the house are hot.

Hot iron

Hot kettle

Hot pan

Hot cup

Hot dish

Hot oven

Hot toaster

What would happen if
you touched them?

Always be careful when you're near hot things.

Fire is another thing that's hot.

Burning flames are very pretty, but can set the house on fire.

Don't play with matches. They're dangerous.

15

Many things in the house
have plugs and wires.

When you plug them in
and switch them on, they begin to work.

These machines run on electricity. Electricity is a kind of power, and helps us in all sorts of ways.

But did you know electricity is dangerous?

Electrical things have different parts.

It's important to leave them all alone.

Never play with electrical things.

Don't touch, Teddy. It could hurt you very badly!

How do you keep your house clean?

Most of us use polish, sprays and other cleaning things.

Household cleaners are very strong.

It's best to stay away from them.
Do you know why?

Don't touch that!
It could hurt
your body.

Medicines are also very strong.
A little medicine can help you
when you are sick.

But too much could make you very ill.

Medicines should always be
locked away.

Even when you're being careful,
accidents sometimes happen.

If Mum or Dad is not around, who do you think could help?

25

Most of the time, your home is safe.

But keep an eye open for danger.

And before you do something that could be risky ...

stop and ask yourself "Is it safe?".

Then, before you know it, you'll be taking care of other people, too!

Notes for parents and teachers

Look Out! At Home and the National Curriculum

This book will help cover elements of the PSHE curriculum at KS1 (ages 5-7), in particular the requirement that children at this age "should be taught rules for, and ways of, keeping safe … and about people who can help them to stay safe." The Citizenship KS1 and KS2 schemes of work are also relevant.

Issues raised in the book

Look Out! At Home is intended to be an enjoyable book that discusses the importance of safety in the home. Throughout, children are given the opportunity to think about taking care of themselves and about what might happen if they don't. It allows them time to explore these issues and discuss them with their family, class and school. It encourages them to think about safety first and about their own responsibility in keeping safe.

The book looks at the things at home that are potentially hazardous – knives, electricity sockets, and matches, for example – and asks questions about the consequences of playing with dangerous things.

It is also full of situations that children and adults will have encountered. It allows a child to ask and answer questions on a one-to-one basis with you. How can you avoid accidents at home? What should you do if things go wrong? Who are the best people to help you if they do? The illustrations help to answer these questions with ideas and suggestions.

Being safe at home is important for everyone. Can your children think of an incident in which they fell down, or burnt themselves on something hot? What happened? How did it feel? The book tackles these and many other issues. It uses open-ended questions to encourage children to think for themselves about the consequences of their behaviour.

Suggested follow-up activities

Make a model of your home and point out areas where there are potential dangers. Discuss the different sort of dangers that might be encountered around the home.

Look at the labels on bottles with your child and see which ones have danger signs.

Think about all the things in the home that use electricity. Now ask your child to draw a sign that means 'Warning – this is dangerous'. Stick it to electrical items around the house to highlight the potential danger.

List all the things that could be hot in your house. Discuss different ways you can avoid getting burnt.

The Royal Society for the Prevention of Accidents (ROSPA) has a useful and informative website including fact sheets: www.rospa.com

Books to read

Look Out at Home (Evans Brothers, 2003)

Safety First At Home (Franklin Watts, 2004)